# What the Bible Says About...

*31 studies on important topics*
———————— AND ————————
*a simple Bible marking plan*

# E. Lonnie Melashenko

**Pacific Press® Publishing Association**
Nampa, Idaho
Oshawa, Ontario, Canada
www.pacificpress.com

Cover design: Michelle C. Petz
Inside design: Steve Lanto


Copyright © 2003 by
Pacific Press® Publishing Association
Printed in the United States of America
All rights reserved


Additional copies of this book may be purchased at
www.adventistbookcenter.com


ISBN: 0-8163-2004-7


03  04  05  06  07 • 5  4  3  2  1

# The Chain Reference Bible Marking Plan

This easy-to-use Bible marking plan will place a wealth of Bible knowledge at your fingertips—either to share with others or for your own personal study and enrichment. By following these simple instructions you can follow key subjects throughout the Bible, learning what God's Word has to say about each important topic. You will be comparing text with text, just as the Bible itself suggests we should do in order to understand God's message. Your Bible will become an encyclopedia of biblical information connected into a series of fascinating Bible studies.

Here's how to go about it.

1. Copy the Bible Study Index on page 8 onto a blank page at the back of your Bible. For each lesson, write the lesson title, the code for that lesson, and the "key text." Use only one line per lesson for recording this information; the result should look the same as the Index on page 8. This will provide the starting point for each of the thirty-one Bible lessons.

2. Next, mark your Bible with the chain-reference texts for each lesson, using the outline provided in this book. For example, Lesson 1—How to Understand the Bible—begins with the key text: John 17:17. Turn to this text in your Bible. Use the appropriate colored pencil and a ruler to draw a vertical line beside this verse in the margin of your Bible. Then lightly highlight the text, or key phrases, with your colored pencil. (As you go through Lesson 1, you will mark each verse in the lesson in the same way and with the same color.)

3. Next, write in the margin beside John 17:17 the code for Lesson 1 and the next text in that series. For example, you would write 2UB 2 Timothy 2:15. This will tell you the next text to look up as you follow Lesson 1.

4. Now turn to 2 Timothy 2:15 and mark it the same way you have marked John 17:17. In the margin you will draw a vertical line in the same color and write, 3UB Isaiah 28:9, 10. This will tell you the third text in the lesson.

5. Continue in this way through Lesson 1, marking each text in the lesson. Beside the last text in Lesson 1, write: UB-End.

6. Mark each of the thirty-one lessons in the same way, using the appropriate color for each lesson.

7. Sometimes, a lesson will contain other Bible references in addition to the main texts to help fill out the point being made. These will be indicated in the lesson with the letters "cf.," meaning "see also." You can include these texts in your marking plan as follows:

   a. In the margin beside the main text to which the additional text refers, write an asterisk (*).

   b. At the bottom of the page in your Bible, write an asterisk like a footnote and list the additional text(s). When studying this lesson, you'll be able to go to this cross-referenced text and then back to the main text to which it refers to continue the study.

   c. If you use the same page again for other lessons, use two asterisks (**) to show which texts go with that lesson.

**Note:** Use colored pencils when marking texts—rather than a felt marking pen or ink—since these can bleed through the paper. I suggest using eight colors to add interest and to be able to easily follow individual lessons. If you follow this eight-color marking system, you will be able to identify easily the general category into which a particular lesson fits.

1. RED for the plan of salvation, restoration, and related subjects. Red signifies the innocent blood of Jesus, shed for the sinner.

2. YELLOW for lessons related to the second coming of Christ. Yellow stands for the brilliance and glory of His appearing.

3. ORANGE for the sanctuary, the 2,300-day prophecy, judgment, and other subjects relating to the sanctuary. Orange reminds us of the gold of the sanctuary.

4. GREEN for Bible prophecy and the Spirit of Prophecy.

5. BLUE for the Ten Commandments, Chrisitian standards, and obedience. Blue symbolizes integrity and consistency.

6. PURPLE for the origin of sin, Satan, man's apostasy, the antichrist, etc. Christ was mocked with a purple robe by His enemies.

7. BROWN for death, hell, the soul, and related subjects. Brown symbolizes the color of dust.

8. BLACK for miscellaneous subjects, promises, and general topics.

# Contents

# Bible Study Index

# How to Understand the Bible

## Lesson 1

*Marking Code: UB*
*Marking Color: Green*
*Key Text: John 17:17*

1. **John 17:17.** The greatest question ever asked is: "What is truth?" Where can we find truth? God's Word, the Bible, is the source of truth.

2. **2 Timothy 2:15.** Correct study is essential to right understanding. How should we study the Bible? Paul tells us to rightly divide (compare, interpret) the word of truth.

3. **Isaiah 28:9, 10.** Comparing scripture with scripture puts truth together like a puzzle—line upon line, here a little and there a little—to form a comprehensive picture of God's truth.

4. **Acts 17:11.** We are to study for ourselves, testing all human teachers and teachings by the Bible. How do we test teachings by the Word?
   - We search the Bible individually for ourselves.
   - We ask God for the guidance of the Holy Spirit (cf. 1 Corinthians 2:13, 14).
   - We build on the study of godly Christian preachers and teachers—going to the Bible to compare their teachings with God's Word (cf. Acts 8:30, 31, 33).

5. **Isaiah 8:20.** This is the litmus test to discern error.

Any teaching that does not harmonize with God's Word—the law and the testimony—is error and contains no light.

6. **2 Timothy 3:15-17.** *All* Scripture is given by God's inspiration and is profitable for our study. The Old Testament (the "Scripture" of Paul's day) as well as the New Testament is God's inspired Word.

7. **1 Corinthians 10:11.** The experiences recorded in the Bible have personal application to our lives. They are written for our admonition.

8. **Luke 24:44, 45.** Jesus endorses the accuracy and inspiration of the Old Testament (The Law, the Prophets, and the Psalms were the three divisions of the Old Testament in His day.)

9. **2 Peter 1:19-21.** Brilliant men with high IQ's did not think up these wonderful Spirit-designed truths. They originated with the moving of the Holy Spirit upon the hearts and minds of holy men of God. The Bible is its own best interpreter.

10. **John 5:39, 40.** To be a Bible "whiz" is not enough. We can search the Bible to accumulate knowledge, but unless we come to know the Christ of the Bible it is of little value.
    • cf. Luke 11:28; John 7:17.

11. **Jeremiah 15:16.** Joy results from following God's Word.

UB-End.

# The Origin of Sin

*Marking Code: OS*
*Marking Color: Purple*
*Key Text: 1 Peter 5:8*

1. **1 Peter 5:8.** The Bible identifies the devil as the adversary of human beings, bent on their spiritual destruction. For other biblical identifications of the devil:
   - cf. Revelation 20:2 (as Satan).
   - cf. Isaiah 14:12 (as Lucifer).
   - cf. John 8:44 (as a murderer and a liar).
   - cf. James 2:19 (there are devil*s* as well as *the* devil).

2. **1 John 3:8.** The devil sinned from the beginning. Those who sin are following his lead and example.

3. **Ezekiel 28:11-19.** These verses are a detailed description of Satan—his original perfection in heaven, his pride resulting in sin, his fall, and ultimate destruction as a result of sin. Satan was perfect when created; sin did not arise due to some defect in the way God created him. Sin is basically unreasonable and without a rational cause.

4. **Isaiah 14:12-15.** The first sin arose out of Lucifer's selfishness and pride.

5. **Revelation 12:7-9.** Satan's sin eventually resulted in open rebellion against God. There was war in

heaven. Satan and his angels fought against Jesus and His angels. Satan and his followers were expelled from heaven to earth.

- cf. Daniel 10:13; Jude 9. Michael is another name for Jesus.
- cf. 2 Peter 2:4; Jude 6. The Bible speaks of angels who sinned—those who followed Satan in rebellion.
- cf. Luke 10:18. Jesus says He saw Satan fall from heaven.
- cf. Revelation 12:4. This text suggests one-third of the angels may have followed Satan's rebellion in heaven.

6. **Genesis 3:1-6.** Satan transported his rebellion from heaven to earth when he deceived Adam and Eve into sin in the Garden of Eden.

7. **1 John 4:16, 18.** Why didn't God destroy evil? Why didn't He destroy Lucifer (or Adam and Eve) when they sinned? Free choice is the key to true love and worship. God wants beings who love and worship Him because they *want* to—not because they are afraid not to!

8. **Hebrews 2:14.** Jesus came to demonstrate His power over the devil and to destroy him.
- cf. Matthew 4:1-11; John 14:30.

9. **Ephesians 6:10-18.** By God's grace, we too can have victory over sin and the devil.
- cf. 1 Corinthians 15:57.

10. **Romans 16:20.** Sin and Satan will come to their end. There is an appointed time for their destruction.

OS-End.

# Steps to Christ

*Marking Code: SC*
*Marking Color: Red*
*Key Text: 1 John 5:13*

1. **1 John 5:13.** The Bible says that we can *know* that we have eternal life. If we believe—and continue to believe in Jesus' name—He has promised that we have eternal life.

2. **Ephesians 2:8, 9.** Can being good save us? No. We are saved by God's grace (unmerited, undeserved favor) as a gift—not by our works.

3. **Romans 3:10, 23.** No one is righteous in himself or herself. Everyone has sinned and fallen short of God's ideal. We see why salvation must be by God's grace and not by our works when we understand what the Bible says about our sinful human nature.
   - cf. Romans 7:21-23. Evil struggles in our human nature against the good.
   - cf. Romans 6:23. The wages of sin is death.
   - cf. Romans 5:12. Death has come to everyone, because everyone sins.
   - cf. Jeremiah 13:23. We cannot change our natures by our own efforts.

4. **Romans 5:6-10.** In spite of our sinfulness, God loves us and wants to give us eternal life. If fact, Christ died for us while we were still sinners.

5. **John 3:16.** God loved us so much He gave His only son Jesus so that everyone who believes on Him should not die, but have everlasting life.
   - cf. 2 Corinthians 5:21—Jesus became sin for us so that we might become righteous in Him.
   - cf. Isaiah 53:6. God laid on Jesus the sins of all human beings.
   - cf. John 14:6. Jesus is the only way to salvation.
   - cf. 1 Peter 2:24. We are healed by His stripes. He bore our sins on the cross.
   - cf. 1 John 5:11. God has given us eternal life in His Son Jesus Christ.
   - cf. Acts 4:12. There is no other name than Jesus by which we may be saved.

6. **John 1:12.** Our part in salvation is to exercise faith in Jesus as our Savior.
   - cf. Ephesians 2:8, 9. We are saved by grace through faith.
   - cf. 1 John 5:12. We have life as long as we have Jesus.

### Our Part

| | |
|---|---|
| Repent | cf. Acts 3:19 |
| Believe | cf. Romans 1:16 |
| Confess/Forsake | cf. Proverbs 28:13 |
| Obey | cf. 1 John 2:3-5 |
| | cf. Hebrews 5:9 |
| | cf. 1 John 3:24 |
| | cf. 1 John 5:2, 3 |
| | cf. John 14:15, 21 |

### God's Part

| | |
|---|---|
| Forgiveness | cf. Isaiah 1:18 |
| Cleansing | cf. 1 John 1:9 |
| New heart | cf. Ezekiel 36:26, 27 |

| New life | cf. 2 Corinthians 5:17 |
| Power | cf. John 1:12 |
| Winning life | cf. Romans 6:6, 14 |
| Eternal life | cf. 1 John 5:11 |

7. **Revelation 3:20.** The most important part is to accept. If we will open the door of our heart, Jesus will come in to live with us.
   - cf. Romans 8:1. There is no condemnation to those who are in Jesus.
   - cf. John 6:47. He who believes in Jesus has everlasting life.

SC-End.

# Christ's Coming

## Lesson 4

*Marking Code: CC*
*Marking Color: Yellow*
*Key Text: John 14:1-3*

1. **John 14:1-3.** Jesus personally promises to come again to take us to be with Him. Some 300 times—approximately one text out of every twenty-five—the New Testament promises that Jesus will return! Some samples include:
   - cf. Matthew 16:27.
   - cf. Matthew 16:64.
   - cf. Hebrews 9:28.
   - cf. Revelation 22:20.

2. **Job 19:25, 26.** The Old Testament, likewise, speaks of Jesus' coming.
   - cf. Psalm 50:3-5.
   - cf. Isaiah 66:15, 16.
   - cf. Daniel 2:44, 45.
   - cf. Jude 14—Enoch, the seventh in descent from Adam, prophesied of Jesus' coming.

3. **1 Thessalonians 4:16, 17.** The New Testament apostles speak of Christ's coming.
   - cf. Titus 2:13.
   - cf. 2 Peter 3:10.

4. **Revelation 22:12.** When Jesus comes again, He will reward each person according to the life's record.

- cf. Matthew 25:31-46.

5. **2 Timothy 4:1.** When Jesus comes again, He will judge the living and the dead.
   - cf. Revelation 6:15-17.

6. **2 Thessalonians 1:7, 8.** When Jesus comes again, He will put an end to sin and sinners.
   - cf. Nahum 1:9.
   - cf. 2 Thessalonians 2:8.

7. **Acts 1:9-11.** Jesus will return literally, in person, with clouds of angels.
   - cf. Revelation 1:7.

8. **Luke 21:27.** Jesus will return with power and great glory.
   - cf. Matthew 24:30, 31, 23-27.

9. **Revelation 6:15-17.** These verses describe the re-action of the wicked to Jesus' coming—and their fate.

10. **Isaiah 25:9.** These verses describe the reaction of the redeemed to Jesus' coming.

11. **Matthew 24:42-44.** "Watch and be ready!" Christ appeals to men and women to be ready whenever Jesus returns.
    - cf. Titus 2:11-14.

CC-End.

# Signs of the Times

*Marking Code: ST*
*Marking Color: Yellow*
*Key Text: Matthew 24:36*

**Note:** This lesson on the *signs* of Christ's return is based primarily on Matthew 24. There are two other major chapters in the Bible dealing entirely with this subject—Mark 13 and Luke 21. Be sure to read and carefully study these chapters as well.

In Matthew 24, Jesus answers two key questions:

- When would the temple in Jerusalem be destroyed? (See verses 1-3; 15-20.)
- When would He return again? (See the rest of Matthew 24.)

1. **Matthew 24: 36.** We cannot set dates for the return of Jesus. No one knows the day or hour of the Second Coming.

2. **Matthew 24:33.** However, by observing the signs that Jesus gives, we *can* know when His coming is near.

3. **Matthew 24—Major signs:**
   - **Matthew 24:1-3; 15-20.** The destruction of Jerusalem in A.D. 70.
   - **Matthew 24:21, 22.** The Dark Ages of tribulation (A.D. 538-1798).
   - **Matthew 24:29.** Footprints in the sky—the "dark day" of May 19, 1780.

- **Matthew 24:29:** Footprints in the sky—the stars fall, November 13, 1833.
  - cf. Joel 2:10, 31; Amos 8:9; Isaiah 13:10; Mark 13:24, 25; Luke 21:25; Acts 2:20; Revelation 6:12, 13.

4. **Matthew 24—Additional significant signs:**
   - **Matthew 24:6, 7.**
   - In the political world there will be wars, political instability, and nationalism with nation against nation.
   - In the natural world there will be earthquakes, pestilence, and famine.
     - cf. Luke 21:10, 11; 1 Thessalonians 5:3; Joel 3:9-12.
   - **James 5:1-8.** In the economic world there will be instability, uncertainty, and strife between the wealthy and the poor.
   - **2 Timothy 3:1-5.** In the moral world there will be corruption, pleasure-seeking, and intense evil.
     - cf. Matthew 24:37-39.
   - **Daniel 12:4.** In the world of knowledge there will be an explosion of information and technology.
   - **2 Peter 3:3, 4.** In the religious world there will be scoffers, skeptics, and a lack of true spirituality.
     - cf. Matthew 24:4, 5, 11; 2 Timothy 4:3, 4.

5. **Revelation 7:1-3.** Why hasn't Jesus come yet? The four angels are continuing to hold back the winds of strife until God's purposes for this earth are complete and His servants have been sealed.

6. **Romans 13:11-14.** Jesus' return is near! The day is at hand! It's time to awake from our sleep and be ready for Jesus to come again.
   - cf. Matthew 24:42-44; 1 Thessalonians 5:1-6.

7. **Luke 21:28, 36.** We see the signs fulfilled; it's time to look up, for our redemption draws near!    ST-End.

# The Millennium

*Marking Code: M*
*Marking Color: Yellow*
*Key Text: John 5:28, 29*

**Note:** The word *millennium* comes from the Latin word *mille,* meaning "thousand," and *annus,* meaning "year." Thus *millennium* is a period of one thousand years. The word *millennium* itself does not appear in the Bible, but Revelation 20 describes a thousand-year time period that begins when Jesus returns the second time.

1. **John 5:28, 29.** Jesus says that *everyone* who is in the grave will eventually be raised—some to the resurrection of life and some to the resurrection of condemnation.

2. **1 Thessalonians 4:16, 17.** Paul describes four classes of people on the earth when Jesus comes—the righteous living, the righteous dead, the wicked living, and the wicked dead. The righteous dead will be raised to life, and the righteous living will be caught up with them to meet Jesus in the air.

3. **2 Thessalonians 2:8.** At Jesus' coming, the wicked living will be destroyed by the brightness of Jesus' coming.

4. **Revelation 20:4-6.** The wicked dead will remain un-

conscious in their graves when Jesus comes. Those who are raised in the "first resurrection"—the righteous—are "blessed and holy." The "rest of the dead"—the wicked—are not raised until the end of the thousand years. They remain sleeping in their graves. There is no second chance at salvation for those who are lost.

5. **Revelation 20:1-3.** Satan is bound to this earth during the millennium—or thousand-year period—following Jesus' second coming.

6. **Jeremiah 4:23-27.** The earth is desolate and uninhabited during the millennium.
   • cf. Jeremiah 25:33.

7. **1 Corinthians 6:2, 3.** The saints judge the world during the thousand years.
   • cf. Revelation 20:4, 6.

8. **Revelation 21:2.** At the end of the millennium, Jesus returns with the righteous and all the inhabitants of heaven. The Holy City, New Jerusalem, descends to earth from heaven.
   • cf. Zechariah 14:3-10.

9. **Revelation 20:3-13.** At the end of the millennium, Satan is loosed for a short time, and the wicked are raised to life to receive their final judgment.

10. **Revelation 20:11, 12.** The wicked stand before God's judgment throne and receive His judgment.
    • cf. Philippians 2:10, 11. Every knee bows before God; every tongue confesses He is righteous. Even the wicked admit that God is just and their sentence is deserved.

11. **Revelation 20:9, 10, 14.** Fire comes down from heaven and destroys forever Satan, his angels, and all the wicked.

12. **Revelation 21:1.** God creates a new earth where righteousness dwells forever.
    • cf. 2 Peter 3:10-13.

    M-End.

# Heaven

*Marking Code: H*
*Marking Color: Yellow*
*Key Text: Isaiah 65:17, 19, 21-25*

**Note:** There are three "heavens" spoken of in the Bible:
- The atmospheric heavens where birds fly (Genesis 1:20; Revelation 19:17).
- The stellar heavens where the planets and stars are located (Genesis 1:14-17; Psalm 19:1).
- Paradise where God lives (2 Corinthians 12:2-4).

This lesson is dealing with the "third" heaven—the home of God and the holy angels—and the place where God will take His redeemed people when Jesus comes.

1. **Isaiah 65:17, 19, 21-25.** The Bible describes heaven as a real place where real people are occupied with real activities that are satisfying and rewarding.

2. **Revelation 7:17.** There will be no tears or mourning in heaven.
   - cf. Isaiah 60:18-20.

3. **Isaiah 11:6-9.** There will be no violence in heaven.

4. **Isaiah 35:1, 2.** The desert will blossom like a rose—all the effects of sin will be ended.
   - cf. Isaiah 51:3.

5. **Hebrews 11:10, 16.** God is building a wonderful city—the New Jerusalem—in heaven for us.

6. **Revelation 21; 22:1-5.** The Bible describes the wonderful city God is preparing—the New Jerusalem—as a place of peace, love, and joy. It will be a place of fellowship with God and Jesus; we will live with Him and be His people.

7. **Zechariah 8:5.** The streets of the city will be filled with boys and girls.

8. **1 Corinthians 13:12.** We will know one another and our loved ones in heaven.
   - cf. John 20:25-28. The disciples recognized Jesus after His resurrection.

9. **Matthew 25:34.** Jesus invites us to inherit the kingdom He has prepared just for us!
   - cf. Revelation 22:14.

H-End.

# Hellfire

*Marking Code: HF*
*Marking Color: Brown*
*Key Text: 2 Peter 3:7, 10-12*

1. **2 Peter 3:7, 10-12.** The Bible is clear that the earth is destined to be destroyed by fire in the day of judgment. Hell is real. But is hell burning now? Is anyone burning in hellfire today? Is the devil doing God's will by being in charge of hell and the torture of the lost? God's reputation—His very character—is at stake in this question of hellfire.

2. **2 Peter 2:9.** The punishment of the unjust (the lost) is reserved until the day of judgment. The wicked do not begin to burn in hell at death.
   - cf. Matthew 13:30, 38-42. The tares are burned at the harvest, at the end of the age.
   - cf. Matthew 25:31-34, 41, 46. The wicked are condemned at the day of judgment when Jesus comes.
   - cf. Revelation 20:7-9, 14; 21:8. Fire destroys Satan, his angels, and the wicked at the end of the millennium.
   - cf. Job 21:30, 32. The wicked wait in their graves for the day of doom.

3. **Malachi 3:11, 12.** The wicked will be burned to ashes—completely destroyed. They will not go on burning throughout eternity.

- cf. Zephaniah 1:18. God will make a "speedy rid-
  dance" of the wicked.

4. **Matthew 3:11, 12.** Doesn't the Bible speak of "unquenchable" fire? Yes. But "unquenchable" fire simply means fire that can't be put out—or "quenched."
   It doesn't mean that the fire won't go out by itself
   when it has consumed everything that is combustible.
   - cf. Jeremiah 17:27; 2 Chronicles 36:19-21. God pre-
     dicted Jerusalem would be burned with "un-
     quenchable" fire due to apostasy. This prediction
     was fulfilled, but that fire is not still burning. It
     could not be put out—until it burned out after
     consuming everything there was to be burned.
   - cf. Jude 7. Likewise, Sodom and Gomorrah suf-
     fered "eternal" fire, but they are not still burning.
     "Eternal" and "everlasting" often mean "as long
     as it is possible for something to last." It is like
     when we say, "I will love you forever." We mean
     "as long as it is possible to love."
   - cf. Jonah 2:6. "Forever" in this case meant "three
     days."
   - cf. 1 Samuel 1:22, 28. "Forever" in this case meant
     for Samuel's lifetime.
   - 2 Thessalonians 1:9. "Everlasting destruction."
     The destruction lasts forever; sinners will never
     live again. But they are not being destroyed for-
     ever—burning forever.

5. **Matthew 10:28.** Jesus said that hell will destroy the
   sinner completely—both body and soul.

6. **Romans 6:23.** The wages of sin is death—not eternal life in hellfire. Eternal life is God's gift to the
   redeemed. In contrast, the end result of sin is death—
   eternal death, never to live again.

7. **Ezekiel 28:18, 19.** Satan himself will be destroyed; he will become ashes and never exist again.
   - cf. Hebrews 2:14.

8. **Nahum 1:9.** Sin itself will be destroyed; it will never arise again.
   - cf. Revelation 21:4.

9. **Ezekiel 33:11.** God has no pleasure in the death of the wicked. For the wicked to burn throughout eternity in hellfire would be torture to a God of love.
   - cf. John 3:16-19.

HF-End.

# Life After Death

*Marking Code: LD*
*Marking Color: Brown*
*Key Text: Job 14:14*

1. **Job 14:14.** What is death? Is it as final as it seems? Or is there something better beyond the tearful goodbyes? If a man dies, will he live again? Men and women have been asking this question as long as death has existed. The Bible has the only source of authoritative information on this important question.

2. **Genesis 2:16, 17; 3:4.** The devil told the first lie to Eve in the Garden of Eden—"You shall not surely die." God had said that death would result if Adam and Eve disobeyed Him and ate the forbidden fruit. But the devil contradicted God. That first lie continues today in the common belief that when a person dies, he or she (a person's soul) continues to live in some form.

3. **Ezekiel 18:4, 20.** Souls *do* die! The Bible often uses the word "soul" to mean simply "a person," "a human being."
   - cf. Matthew 10:28. The soul can be destroyed.

4. **1 Timothy 1:17; 6:15, 16.** Only God is immortal.

5. **1 Corinthians 15:51-54.** Human beings receive immortality only at Jesus' second coming.

6. **Matthew 24:23, 24.** The last days will be a time of deception. Satan is particularly eager to deceive us regarding what happens after death because a misunderstanding here opens the way for him to introduce a multitude of deceptions.
   - cf. Leviticus 20:27. God warns us against consulting those who claim to be able to communicate with the dead.

7. **Ecclesiastes 9:5, 6.** What happens to a person when he or she dies? The Bible is clear that when a person dies, they know nothing. They cease to exist; their feelings and emotions come to an end; they have no part in what happens on earth.
   - cf. Psalm 146:3, 4. Their thoughts perish.
   - cf. Psalm 115:17. The dead do not praise God.

8. **Acts 2:34.** Peter specifically says that David (who had died centuries earlier) had not gone to heaven.

9. **Ecclesiastes 12:7.** When a person dies his or her body returns to dust, and the "spirit" returns to God. What is this "spirit," and what does it mean that it returns to God?

10. **Genesis 2:7.** At Creation, God made Adam out of the dust of the earth (the body) and breathed into him the breath (spirit) of life. The result of this combination is a "living being" (some translations of the Bible say, a "living soul." So body + God's life-giving spirit = a living human being. At death, the process is reversed. The body returns to the earth; God takes back His life-giving spirit; and the living soul—or living being—ceases to exist. Nowhere in the Bible is the word "soul" used to mean a conscious, intelligent entity, capable of existence apart from the body.

11. **Luke 23:42, 43.** Didn't Jesus tell the repentant thief on the cross that he would go to heaven with Him that very day when he and Jesus died? Actually, Jesus didn't go to Paradise that very day of the crucifixion—Friday. He told Mary on Sunday morning—two days later—that He hadn't yet ascended to His Father in heaven (cf. John 20:17). Jesus was assuring the thief, "I tell you this very day when all seems to be failure that you will be with me in heaven." He didn't tell him that they would be in heaven that very day; Jesus told him that very day that they would be together someday in heaven.

12. **1 Thessalonians 4:16-18.** Good News! The righteous people who have died will live again—when Jesus returns. Until then, they sleep in the grave—unconscious, waiting for their Lord to raise them to immortal life.

LD-End.

# Angels

*Marking Code: A*
*Marking Color: Black*
*Key Text: Hebrews 1:13, 14*

1. **Hebrews 1:13, 14.** Angels are God's ministering messengers whom He sends to us to bless us and minister to our needs.

2. **Genesis 3:24.** Angels are not the spirits of dead loved ones. They existed before the first human being died.
   - cf. Job 38:3-7; Psalm 8:4, 5.

3. **Ezekiel 28:14, 15.** Angels are created beings. Lucifer was the highest of the angels, the "anointed cherub." God created him perfect and holy, but he allowed sin to enter his heart.
   - cf. Colossians 1:16.

4. **Ezekiel 10:9, 12.** Angels are not phantoms. They have form and body.
   - cf. Genesis 19:1-3; 18:6-8; John 20:12; Ezekiel 1:14.

5. **Luke 20:35, 36.** Someday, we will have glorious bodies similar to the angels.

6. **Revelation 5:11.** There are more angels than there are people.
   - cf. Hebrews 12:22.

- **Note:** Some Bible scholars believe that redeemed human beings will replace the vacancies left by the angels that followed Lucifer and were cast out of heaven.

7. **Matthew 18:10.** Each of us has a guardian angel assigned to attend us.
   - cf. Acts 12:15.

8. **Psalm 34:7.** Angels protect us from danger during our journey through life.
   - cf. Psalm 91:11, 12; Daniel 6:22; 2 Kings 6:16, 17.

9. **Isaiah 6:2.** There are different orders of angels— the Bible mentions cherubim and seraphim. Some apparently have wings or even multiple wings.
   - cf. Ezekiel 28:14.

10. **Matthew 25:31.** All the angels of heaven will accompany Jesus when He returns to earth the second time.

11. **Matthew 24:31.** At Jesus' coming, the angels will gather together the redeemed from all over the world.

   A-End.

# The Law of God (Ten Commandments)

## *Lesson 11*

*Marking Code: TC*
*Marking Color: Blue*
*Key Text: Exodus 20:1-17*

1. **Exodus 20:1-17.** God gave His moral law, the Ten Commandments, on Mount Sinai. These ten rules for living are an expression of God's character. They tell us how to relate to Him and to each other in a way that is in harmony with God's character of love.

2. **Matthew 5:17-19.** Jesus did not come to destroy—or do away with—the law; He came to fulfill it—live out its principles in His life on earth. He specifically says that God's law will remain as long as heaven and earth exist.
   - cf. Isaiah 42:21. Jesus came to magnify the law and honor it.

3. **Romans 5:12-14.** God's law has always existed, otherwise there could be no sin—or death.
   - cf. Romans 4:15.
   - cf. 1 John 3:4. Sin is "lawlessness" or transgression of the law.
   - cf. Romans 6:23. The penalty for sin is death.

4. **Psalm 19:7.** God's law is perfect and eternal. In this way, it is a reflection of God Himself.
   - cf. Psalm 111:7, 8.

5. **James 2:10-12.** In the final judgment, human beings will be judged by the standard of God's law.
   • cf. James 4:17.

6. **John 14:15.** We keep God's law because we love Him and because He has saved us by His grace. Commandment keeping is *not* a means of salvation. We are not saved by our obedience to God's law. Our obedience is an *evidence* of our salvation.
   • cf. Romans 3:28.
   • cf. John 15:10, 14.
   • cf. 1 John 5:2, 3.
   • cf. Romans 13:10.

7. **1 John 2:3, 4.** The Bible uses strong language to describe those who claim to be God's children but who are disobedient to His commandments. Those who know God and love Him will be willing to obey Him in all things. They are not perfect, but they have an attitude of willing obedience.
   • cf. Proverbs 28:9.

8. **Jeremiah 31:33.** Christ wants to write His law in our hearts. That is, He wants its principles to become a part of our lives so that we obey because we want to obey—not because we feel we must.
   • cf. Psalm 119:1, 10, 165.

9. **Revelation 22:14.** God pronounces a special blessing on those who keep His commandments.

   TC-End.

# Law and Grace

## Lesson 12

*Marking Code: LG*
*Marking Color: Blue*
*Key Text: Ephesians 2:8, 9*

1. **Ephesians 2:8, 9.** The Bible is clear that we are saved by God's grace, through our faith in Him and His saving sacrifice—not by our works or obedience to God's law. Salvation is God's gift to us by His grace.

2. **Acts 4:12.** Sometimes we hear individuals say that human beings were once saved by obedience to the law (in Old Testament times), but that on this side of the Cross we are saved by grace alone. The Bible disagrees! No one is saved by the law—or ever has been. Jesus is the only source of salvation for sinners.
   - cf. Romans 5:18-21. As soon as Adam sinned, grace abounded to sinners.

3. **Romans 6:12-15.** Paul says that Christians are not "under law but under grace" (verse 14). Some have interpreted this verse to mean that before the Cross individuals were saved by the law—by their obedience to it—but that after the Cross we are under grace and have no obligation to keep God's law. How do we reconcile Paul's "problem" statement with the Bible teaching that salvation is by grace and always has been?

4. **Matthew 5:17-19.** Jesus says that He did not come to destroy the law and that the law will last as long

as heaven and earth itself. So the law must have an important function—even if it is not the source of our salvation.

**Note:** There are at least three types of "law" mentioned in the Bible:
- Civil law. These dealt with the government and society of the nation of Israel. cf. Exodus 22:1.
- Ceremonial law. These dealt with the religious, sacrificial services of the temple and worship of Israel. They were temporary and were designed to point forward to the work of Jesus as the Messiah and Lamb of God. cf. Leviticus 4:27-31.
- God's moral law—the Ten Commandments. These are permanent expressions of God's character and remain valid for all peoples and all times. cf. Exodus 32:15, 16; Deuteronomy 10:3, 4, 5; 2 Chronicles 5:10. Paul endorsed the fact that they are permanent expressions of God's will for us. cf. Romans 7:7, 12, 14, 22.

5. **1 John 3:4.** Sin is lawlessness—or the transgression of the law, breaking the law.

6. **Romans 6:23.** The "wages"—the result—of sin is death, eternal death.

7. **Romans 8:1-4.** In these verses, Paul gives us the proper relationship between law and grace—and provides the "solution" to his statement in Romans 6:14 that we are not under law, but under grace. Paul says that we are not under the condemnation of the law of sin and death. God's grace has set us free from the *condemnation* of the law. But we now live so that the righteous requirements of the law might be fulfilled in us—not *to be* saved, but in love and gratitude that we *have been* saved.

8. **Romans 7:7, 8.** The problem is not with the law; it is with our sinful nature! Paul is clear that grace does not do away with God's law.
   - cf. Romans 6:15.

9. **Ephesians 2:14-16.** The ceremonial laws of sacrifices and temple ritual are no longer valid for God's people because the reality they pointed forward to—Jesus' sacrifice—has taken place.
   - cf. Colossians 2:16, 17.
   - cf. Galatians 5:1.
   - cf. Daniel 9:27.

10. **Romans 1:5.** One purpose of God's grace is to enable His saved people to be obedient.
   - cf. Romans 2:13; 16:26.

LG-End.

# Once Saved, Always Saved

## Lesson 13

*Marking Code: AS*
*Marking Color: Red*
*Key Text: Galatians 5:4*

1. **Galatians 5:4.** The question is: Can a person who has received salvation and God's gift of eternal life fall from grace and be lost? Paul says clearly that it is possible. A person may fall from grace.

2. **Hebrews 3:8-15.** Having once known God's truth does not prevent a person from hardening his or her heart against it and rebelling against God.

3. **Hebrews 6:4-6.** Once a person backslides by persistently rejecting God, it is very difficult—almost impossible—to regain a saved relationship with Him.

4. **Hebrews 12:15.** The Bible clearly warns that we can "fall short of the grace of God."

5. **2 Peter 2:20, 21.** The Bible says that it is better for a person never to have known the way of righteousness than to go back to a life of slavery to sin after having known Christ.

6. **Ezekiel 18:24, 26.** When a righteous person falls from grace, all of his or her former righteousness and obedience is not taken into account. Apart from grace, he or she will die for the sins committed.

7. **1 John 2:3, 4.** If a person claims to be saved by grace and yet ignores the law and his need to be obedient to God's will, he is a "liar" and has no truth in him.
   • cf. Romans 6:1, 2.

8. **Hosea 14:4.** God wants to heal our backsliding. If we repent, He will always forgive. Yes, a person can fall from grace by repeatedly disobeying God or deliberately turning away from Him. But God will always accept sincere repentance—and forgive.

AS-End.

# The Bible Sabbath

## Lesson 14

*Marking Code: S*
*Marking Color: Blue*
*Key Text: Revelation 1:10*

1. **Revelation 1:10.** The Lord has a day that belongs to Him, that is His day—the Lord's day. This text doesn't tell us what that day is, but obviously the Lord's day is not just *any* day. The Lord has a special day.

2. **Matthew 12:8.** Jesus is Lord of the Sabbath day. So the Lord's day is the Sabbath day. However, this text still doesn't tell us which day is the Sabbath day.

3. **Exodus 20:8-11.** The seventh day of the week is the Sabbath—the Lord's day. It is the weekly birthday of our world!

4. **Genesis 2:1-3.** God made the Sabbath at the creation of our world, long before there was Jew or Gentile. So the Sabbath belongs to all humanity, not to any one race of people. God did three things to make the Sabbath His special day: He rested on it; He blessed it; and He sanctified it—set it apart for a holy use.

5. **Colossians 1:14-17.** Jesus is the Creator of Genesis. He made our world and everything in it. Jesus is the One who made the Sabbath in the beginning.
   - cf. John 1:10; Mark 2:27, 28; Hebrews 1:1, 2; Ephesians 3:9.

6. **Luke 4:16.** While on earth, Jesus kept the Sabbath.

7. **Luke 23:54–24:1.** At His crucifixion, our Creator-Redeemer rested on the Sabbath from His finished work of salvation just as He had rested on the seventh-day Sabbath at Creation after He finished His work.

8. **Matthew 24:15-20.** Jesus predicted continued Sabbath observance following His death and resurrection. He spoke of the Sabbath in connection with the destruction of Jerusalem that took place forty years later.

9. **Acts 17:2.** Paul kept the Sabbath during his ministry as an ongoing practice. He had no doubt as to which day of the week was the Sabbath. In fact, the book of Acts records repeated instances of the apostles worshiping on the seventh-day Sabbath.
   • cf. Acts 13:14, 42, 44; 16:13; 18:4.

10. **Ezekiel 20:12, 20.** The Sabbath is a sign of our salvation and redemption.
    • cf. Hebrews 4:1-11.

11. **Isaiah 66:22, 23.** In the new earth, after sin has been destroyed, the redeemed will worship on the Sabbath just as Adam and Eve did before sin arose in the Garden of Eden.

12. **Revelation 22:14.** God is leading earnest Christians back to *all* of His commandments. A rebellious people were separated from the tree of life in the Garden of Eden when sin came. An obedient people will be given access to the tree of life in Paradise when sin is done away with forever.

S-End.

# Sunday in the Bible

## Lesson 15

*Marking Code: SB*
*Marking Color: Black*
*Key Text: John 14:21, 23*

1. **John 14:21, 23.** We show our love for Jesus by our willingness to keep His commandments and be obedient to Him. This is as true in the matter of the day He has asked us to keep holy as it is in any other of His commandments.

   **Note:** There are only eight texts in the New Testament that mention the first day of the week—the day we know as Sunday. We will look at each of these eight to determine if any of them tell us that we are to observe Sunday as a holy day or as the Sabbath of the Lord. (Genesis 1:5 is almost the only text in the Old Testament that mentions the first day of the week; it refers to the events of the first day of Creation.)

2. **Matthew 28:1.** This verse tells us that the women came to Jesus' tomb early on the first day of the week. It says nothing about the first day being holy or the Sabbath. In fact, it says that they came "after the Sabbath" on the first day of the week. So the Sabbath was finished before the first day of the week began.

3. **Mark 16:1, 2.** Mark mentions the same event—the women coming to Jesus' tomb on the first day of the

week. He, too, says that Sabbath "was past" when the first day of the week began.

4. **Mark 16:9.** Later that same day—Resurrection Sunday—Jesus appeared to Mary Magdalene. But He said nothing to her about Sunday now being a holy day.

5. **Luke 23:50-56; 24:1.** Luke records the same event told by Matthew and Mark—the appearance of the women at Jesus' tomb early Sunday morning. Like them, Luke says nothing about Sunday now being a holy day.

6. **John 20:1.** This is John's version of the same story already told by Matthew, Mark, and Luke.

7. **John 20:19.** Jesus appeared to the disciples in the evening of that same day—Resurrection Sunday. Some individuals have said that this was a religious service being held because Sunday was now the holy day of worship following the Resurrection. But notice that the disciples were hiding in fear of their lives; they were not holding a worship service.

8. **Acts 20:7, 8.** Paul preached at Troas on the first day of the week—continuing until midnight. This was a special farewell meeting, and the book of Acts records numerous instances of Paul worshiping on the Sabbath. One religious service on Sunday does not make the day holy. Christians often meet for mid-week services on Wednesday or another day—without making that day holy.

9. **1 Corinthians 16:1, 2.** Some have said that these verses refer to taking up an offering in church on the

first day of the week. However, notice that Paul tells the Christians that they are to set aside something on the first day of the week and store it up until he comes. This is practical instruction on beginning to save early in the week at home so that a person didn't have to wait until Paul arrived to determine what he could contribute.

**Note:** These are all the verses in the New Testament that refer to the first day of the week. As we have seen, there is no indication that the Sabbath has been changed from the seventh day of the week to the first day of the week following Jesus' resurrection.

10. **Mark 7:7-13.** Jesus says that if we set aside a commandment of God to follow a man-made tradition, then our worship is in vain.

11. **Colossians 2:12.** Baptism—not Sunday worship—is the memorial of Christ's resurrection.

   SB-End.

# The Change of the Sabbath

*Marking Code: CS*
*Marking Color: Black*
*Key Text: Ecclesiastes 3:14*

**Note:** There was no question in the time of Christ and the apostles as to which day was the Sabbath. Since the Bible plainly states that the seventh day, Saturday, is the Sabbath, why do the majority of Christians keep the first day of the week? How did it change?

1. **Ecclesiastes 3:14.** When God does something, it stands forever.
   - cf. Psalm 89:34; Isaiah 40:8; Malachi 3:6; Matthew 5:17-19.

2. **Daniel 7:25.** Bible prophecy predicts that a power would arise that would intend to change times and laws. The Sabbath commandment is the only one of the Ten Commandments that deals with time.
   - cf. 2 Thessalonians 2:3, 4.

**Note:** Since the New Testament gives no hint of a change from the seventh-day Sabbath to Sunday, we must turn to history and prophecy. Note in outline form these steps in apostasy resulting in the change of the Sabbath from the seventh day of the week to the first day:

   - A.D. 132-135. Jews were discredited and persecuted by Rome as a result of the Bar Kochba revolt.

Christians became increasingly sensitive to any identification of themselves with Jews. The seventh-day Sabbath was one thing both Jews and Christians had in common.

- Christians began to minimize Sabbath keeping. Many Christians had been pagan sun-worshipers before their conversion to Christ. They had honored the first day of the week—the "sun day." They began to reason that if they adopted some of the pagan customs, Christianity would have more appeal to pagans.

- Sunday first came into the Christian church as a holiday, not as a day of worship. Then for centuries, both the first day and the seventh day were observed. However, under the influence of paganism and persecution, Sunday became emphasized, and the seventh-day Sabbath was minimized.

- A.D. 321. Emperor Constantine decreed that all government offices, courts, and artisans' shops be closed on the first day of the week—the "venerable day of the sun."

- A.D. 364. The Council of Laodicea (Canon 29) stipulated that the church had changed the day of rest from the seventh day to the first day of the week.

**Note:** Both Protestants and Catholics acknowledge this change:

- ***Roman Catholic.*** "The church. . . substituted the observance of Sunday. . . for the observance of Saturday. . . a change for which there is no Scriptural authority" (Stephen Keenan, *A Doctrinal Catechism,* p. 174).

- ***Roman Catholic.*** "You may read the Bible from Genesis to Revelation, and you will not find a single line authorizing the sanctification of Sunday. The Scriptures enforce the religious observance of Saturday, a day which we never sanctify"

(Cardinal Gibbon, *The Faith of Our Fathers,* p. 89).

- *Lutheran.* "They [Roman Catholics] allege the Sabbath changed into Sunday, the Lord's day, contrary to the Decalogue, as it appears. . . The Church dispensed with one of the Ten Commandments" (*Augsburg Confession,* article XXVIII).

- *Methodist.* "There is no positive command. . . for keeping holy the first day of the week" (Amos Binney, *Theological Compendium,* pp. 180, 181).

- *Congregationalist:* "It is quite clear that however rigidly or devoutly we may spend Sunday, we are not keeping the Sabbath" (R. W. Dale, *The Ten Commandments,* pp. 106, 107).

- *Presbyterian.* "The moral law doth forever bind us all. . . . Neither doth Christ in the gospel any way dissolve, but much strengthens this obligation" (*The Constitution of the Presbyterian Church in the USA*).

- *Church of England.* "There is no word, no hint in the New Testament about abstaining from work on Sunday. . . . Into the rest of Sunday no divine law enters" (Canon Eyton, *The Ten Commandments*).

3. **Matthew 15:9.** Jesus warns of worship that follows human traditions rather than the doctrines of God. He says that such worship is in vain.

4. **Isaiah 58:12-14.** The Bible speaks of those who would bring about a restoration of God's holy Sabbath.

5. **John 9:41.** God does not condemn us when we break His commandments in ignorance or unknowingly.
   - cf. James 4:17.

6. **Acts 5:29.** When we understand the issues, we should obey God rather than the commandments of men.
   - cf. Romans 6:16.                    CS-End.

# How to Keep the Sabbath

## Lesson 17

*Marking Code: KS*
*Marking Color: Blue*
*Key Text: Exodus 20:8-10*

1. **Exodus 20:8-10.** True Sabbath keeping includes physical as well as spiritual rest. We are to cease all our regular labor and occupations in order to enter into fellowship with God.

2. **Isaiah 66:22, 23.** The Sabbath includes spiritual rest and fellowship. Sinless Adam and Eve didn't need physical rest as much as they needed to cease from their own interests and pursuits in order to spend quality time with God. This will be one of the reasons for Sabbath keeping in the earth made new.

3. **Leviticus 23:32.** The Sabbath begins at sunset on Friday and ends at sunset on Saturday. At Creation, the evening preceded the morning of each day (cf. Genesis 1:5, 8, 13). According to the Bible, each day begins and ends at sunset.

4. **Mark 15:42.** The Bible calls the day before the Sabbath, the "preparation day." Friday is the day to prepare for the Sabbath.
   - cf. Exodus 16:22, 23. The baking and cooking are to be done.

5. **Isaiah 58:12-14.** We are to turn our feet away from

trampling on God's holy Sabbath by engaging in common business transactions. Rather we are to make the Sabbath a day of joy!

- cf. Jeremiah 17:21, 22. Bear no burdens on the Sabbath; no work.
- cf. Luke 23:56. Rest on the Sabbath.
- cf. Exodus 34:21. Don't plow or harvest.
- cf. Nehemiah 13:15-22. Don't buy or sell anything.
- cf. Isaiah 56:2, 6, 7. Don't pollute the Sabbath.

6. **Matthew 12:10-12.** We can do good on the Sabbath—this includes all kinds of activities that help others and that build morality, integrity, and spirituality in us and our families—that draw us closer to God and to one another. Suggestions:

- cf. Leviticus 23:3. Rest physically and spiritually.
- cf. Proverbs 22:6. Teach our children spiritual values and interact with them.
- cf. Isaiah 40:26. See God's works in nature.
- cf. Isaiah 66:22, 23. Worship God.
- cf. Matthew 24:14. Preach, teach, and spread the good news of Jesus.
- cf. Matthew 25:35, 36. Help the needy, feed the hungry, visit those in prison.
- cf. Luke 4:16. Attend worship services at church.
- cf. Luke 13:14-17. Do good to all God's creatures.
- cf. Acts 17:11. Study God's Word and fortify your mind with His truth.

7. **Deuteronomy 5:15.** We are to keep the Sabbath as a sign of our redemption by God from the slavery of sin.

- cf. Ezekiel 20:12, 20.
- cf. Mark 2:27, 28.

KS-End.

# Tithing

## Lesson 18

*Marking Code: T*
*Marking Color: Blue*
*Key Text: Psalm 50:10-12*

1. **Psalm 50:10-12.** The world and everything in it belongs to God. He is the owner of everything.

2. **Deuteronomy 8:17, 18.** This is an example of the pagan theory of ownership. This theory says that whatever you have the power to take, belongs to you.

3. **1 Corinthians 4:2.** This is the Christian theory of ownership. We own nothing; rather, we are stewards—or managers—of what God gives to us. We are to be faithful caretakers of what He entrusts to us.

4. **1 Timothy 6:10.** It is not money that is evil, but the love of money—greed and the craving for more.

5. **Exodus 20:8-11.** God claims one-seventh of our time—the Sabbath—as His.

6. **Leviticus 27:30-33.** God claims one-tenth of our income—the tithe—as His. The tithe is holy, just as the Sabbath is holy. God is testing our selfishness just as He tested Adam and Eve. He asked them not to eat of a particular tree. He asks us for one-seventh of our time (the Sabbath) and one-tenth of our income (the tithe). One out of every two parables

Jesus told was about money. This subject is important because human beings are basically selfish. God wants to remove selfishness from our hearts through faithful stewardship of our time and money.

7. **Genesis 14:18-20.** The tithe was instituted by God long before the Mosaic laws were given to Israel.
   - cf. Genesis 28:20-22.

8. **Numbers 18:20-24.** The tithe is to be used to support the gospel ministry.
   - cf. 1 Corinthians 9:13, 14.

9. **Matthew 23:23.** Jesus endorsed the tithing principle.

10. **Malachi 3:8-11.** The tithe is to be placed in the church treasury for the support of God's work.
    - cf. Nehemiah 13:10-13.

11. **2 Corinthians 9:7.** The motive or attitude with which we respond to God's call to be stewards is important. God wants us to give cheerfully because we love Him.

12. **Malachi 3:10-12.** If we are faithful in our stewardship, God promises to bless us abundantly. His promises are sure.
    - cf. Proverbs 3:9, 10.
    - Luke 6:38; 16:10-12.

13. **Matthew 6:19-21.** Jesus urges us to store up treasure in heaven—rather than trying to amass treasure on earth.

    T-End.

# Healthful Living

*Marking Code: HL*
*Marking Color: Blue*
*Key Text: 3 John 2*

1. **3 John 2.** God wants us to prosper physically and be in health just as much as He wants us to prosper spiritually. God communicates to us through the channel of our minds, so it is important that we have healthy bodies and clear minds.

2. **Romans 12:1, 2.** God's request that we keep our bodies healthy for His service is a "reasonable" expectation. Likewise, His guidelines for keeping us healthy are also logical and reasonable.
   • cf. Galatians 6:7.

3. **1 Corinthians 6:19, 20.** Our bodies belong to God, therefore they are "holy" and should be treated as such.

4. **1 Corinthians 3:16, 17.** We can defile the temple of our bodies by unhealthful practices—including what we eat and drink.
   • cf. Daniel 1:8.

5. **Isaiah 55:2.** God commands us to eat only those foods that are good for us.

6. **Genesis 1:29.** The original diet God gave human beings included fruits, nuts, and grains.

- cf. Genesis 3:17, 18. Vegetables were added later, after sin came into the world.

7. **Genesis 9:1-4.** Following the Flood, God allowed human beings to eat flesh food.

8. **Leviticus 11:1-20.** God carefully defines "clean" and "unclean" animals—those that may be eaten and those that may not.
   - Genesis 7:2. This distinction between "clean" and "unclean" animals was delineated at the time of the Flood—long before the Mosaic ceremonial laws.
   - cf. Deuteronomy 14:2-20.

9. **Proverbs 20:1.** The Bible urges God's people to abstain from alcoholic beverages—including wine.
   - cf. 1 Corinthians 6:10. Drunkards will not inherit the kingdom of God.
   - cf. 1 Timothy 5:23. This text is referring to medicine; it is not recommending drinking alcohol.

10. **Revelation 21:27.** Heaven will not contain anything that defiles or corrupts. This would certainly include recreational drugs, tobacco in all its forms, and other unhealthful practices.

11. **1 Corinthians 10:31.** Whatever we do, we are to do everything in a way that will glorify God—and that includes what we eat or drink.

HL-End.

# Right Standards

## Lesson 20

*Marking Code: RS*
*Marking Color: Blue*
*Key Text: Philippians 4:8*

1. **Philippians 4:8.** Those who love Jesus will want to please Him in all things. They will not want to do anything that will destroy or harm their relationship of love and trust with Him.

2. **Galatians 5:22-24.** Excess in anything is sin. Moderation, temperance, and self-control are the Holy Spirit's ideal for us.
   • cf. Philippians 3:18, 19.

3. **2 Timothy 2:15.** We are to conduct ourselves in a way that God can approve. Anything immoral or spiritually offensive—whether it be presented in a movie, book, theater play, or music—is inappropriate for the Christian.

4. **2 Corinthians 6:14.** Christian standards include faithfulness to God and each other in the marriage relationship.
   • cf. Matthew 5:27, 28; 19:9.

5. **1 Timothy 2:9.** Christian standards require propriety in the way we dress. Modesty and simplicity are the two basic principles.

6. **Deuteronomy 22:5.** Clothing should be neat, clean, and appropriately tailored for the gender, culture, and occasion.
   • cf. Ecclesiastes 9:8.

7. **Isaiah 3:16-23.** Because of pride, the Bible warns against the free use of ornamental jewelry and colorful cosmetics.

   **Note:** Throughout the Bible, spiritual reformation is always accompanied by dress reform and the removal of ornamental jewelry. cf. Genesis 35:1-5; Exodus 33:5, 6; Hosea 2:13.

8. **1 Peter 3:3-5.** It is the inner person that counts—not the external adornment.

9. **1 John 2:15-17.** The Bible counsels us not to love the world and its glitter. All the pride of the world will pass away.

10. **2 Corinthians 7:1.** We are to perfect holiness, avoiding anything that would defile us spiritually or separate us from God.

11. **Philippians 4:13.** Through Christ, we can do anything He wants us to do.

   RS-End.

# The Sanctuary

*Marking Code: TS*
*Marking Color: Orange*
*Key Text: Exodus 25:8, 9, 40*

1. **Exodus 25:8, 9, 40.** God directed His Old Testament people to build a sanctuary as a place where He could dwell with them. Its symbols and rituals were designed to point forward to the Lamb of God and His atoning ministry. It was the gospel in miniature thousands of years before Christ came. By studying the sanctuary service, we will find that the plan of salvation becomes electrifyingly clear.

2. **Hebrews 9.** The two apartments (or rooms) of the sanctuary—the Holy Place and the Most Holy Place—represent phases of Christ's ministry. The Holy Place corresponds to His earthly ministry, and the Most Holy Place corresponds to His heavenly ministry. Each room had furniture that represented the activities of its phase of ministry.

3. **Hebrews 8:1.** The priest in the sanctuary service represented Jesus, our High Priest.

4. **Hebrews 9:12.** The blood of the animals that were offered as sacrifices represented the blood of Jesus.

5. **John 8:12; Revelation 1:20.** The candlestick, or

lamp stand, in the Holy Place represented Jesus, the Light of the world, and His church.

6. **John 6:35; 48-63.** The "showbread" in the Holy Place represented Jesus, the Bread of Life, and His word.

7. **Revelation 8:3, 4.** The incense offered in the Holy Place represented the prayers of God's people.

8. **Leviticus 4:27-31.** The daily service in the Holy Place represented the plan of redemption and Christ's sacrifice at Calvary. Sin was symbolically transferred from the sinner to the sacrificial animal. Jesus daily intercedes for us and applies His blood to cover our sins.
   • cf. Hebrews 8:1-5; 7:25; 9:24.

9. **Leviticus 16:4-22.** The yearly service took place once each year on the Day of Atonement in the Most Holy Place. It was a day of judgment when the sins that had symbolically accumulated in the sanctuary throughout the year were cleansed. It represented the heavenly ministry of Jesus—the judgment.

10. **Matthew 27:51.** When Christ's sacrifice as the Lamb of God was completed, the veil separating the two rooms in the sanctuary was torn apart from top to bottom. This signified that the sacrifice was complete and that the human priesthood and sanctuary services had fulfilled their purpose. Then Jesus took His place as our High Priest in heaven. cf. Hebrews 8:1, 2.

11. **Hebrews 9:25, 26.** Jesus entered the Most Holy Place of the sanctuary in heaven once in the last days of the world. This heavenly ministry was symbolized

by the yearly service of the sanctuary on earth when the high priest entered the Most Holy Place once each year on the Day of Atonement.

12. **Revelation 22:11.** When Jesus leaves His work as our High Priest in the Most Holy Place of the heavenly sanctuary, the destiny of every person will be sealed for eternity.

13. **Isaiah 43:25.** We need to let Jesus blot out our sins while His ministry in heaven is still going forward.

   TS-End.

# The 2,300-Day Prophecy

*Marking Code: TD*
*Marking Color: Green*
*Key Text: Daniel 8:13, 14*

1. **Daniel 8:13, 14.** In vision, Daniel heard that the sanctuary would be cleansed after 2,300 "days."

   **Note:** The 2,300-day prophetic period graphically outlines with unerring accuracy the very time when the Messiah was to arrive, the number of years He was to spend in ministry, the time of His crucifixion, and His inauguration as our high priest in the heavenly sanctuary. The event that takes place at the end of the 2,300 "days" is of vital interest to every human being. That is when the great judgment day begins and Christ carries out His final ministry for human beings.

2. **Daniel 8:1-27.** Daniel saw in vision the rise and fall of empires—Medo-Persia, Greece, and Rome. He saw the rise of a religious-political power that would trample on God's people, the sanctuary, its priesthood, sacrifice, and altar. Daniel raises the crucial question: "How long will truth be trampled to the ground?" The answer is for 2,300 days—and then the sanctuary will be cleansed.

3. **Numbers 14:34.** In Bible time prophecies, a prophetic "day" equals a literal year of actual time.

4. **Daniel 9:1-3, 20-24.** An angel explains to Daniel that 70 weeks—490 years—were to be "cut off" from the 2,300 days as probationary time for the Jewish nation.

5. **Daniel 9:25.** The 70 weeks and the 2,300 days were to begin with the command to restore and rebuild Jerusalem. This decree was issued by Artaxerxes in 457 B.C.
   - cf. Ezra 6:14; 7:7, 11-13.

6. **Daniel 9:25.** The 70 weeks were to be subdivided into seven weeks and 62 weeks. Seven weeks—49 years—from 457 B.C. brings us to 408 B.C., when the temple at Jerusalem was rebuilt.

7. **Daniel 9:25.** Messiah the Prince was to come after 69 weeks—483 years. This would extend to the year A.D. 27. Jesus was anointed by His baptism in the autumn of A.D. 27 exactly on time with the prophecy!
   - cf. Mark 1:14, 15. Jesus began His ministry by saying that the "time is fulfilled"—the time predicted by the prophecy of Daniel for the Messiah to appear.
   - cf. Acts 10:37, 38. Jesus was anointed at His baptism.

8. **Daniel 9:26, 27.** One week—seven years—still remained for the Jewish nation. This would be the period from A.D. 27 to A.D. 34. Messiah was to be cut off and cause the sacrifice to cease in the "middle of the week." Jesus was crucified in the spring of A.D. 31—exactly three-and-a-half years from His baptism in the autumn of A.D. 27.

**Note:** There would be 1,810 more years until the end of the 2,300-year prophecy, at which time Christ was to leave the first room (the Holy Place) of the heavenly sanctuary and begin His final ministry for humanity in the second room (the Most Holy Place). Adding 1,810 years to A.D. 34 brings us to A.D. 1844. According to the prophecy of Daniel 8:13, 14, this date marks the beginning of the "cleansing" of the sanctuary— or the judgment in heaven.

9. **Hebrews 9:11-15.** This cleansing—or work of judgment—takes place in the sanctuary in heaven.

TD-End.

# The Judgment

*Marking Code: J*
*Marking Color: Black*
*Key Text: Romans 14:10-12*

1. **Romans 14:10-12.** Every human being must stand before the judgment seat of Christ. It is a solemn event, but we don't need to be afraid because our judge is Jesus, who loves us and died for us.
   • cf. 2 Corinthians 5:10.

2. **Acts 17:31.** God has appointed a day for the judgment. There is a definite time when the judgment will take place.

3. **Revelation 14:7.** In the last days, the first angel announces to the world that the hour of God's judgment "has come."

4. **Daniel 7:9, 10.** In vision, Daniel saw the judgment taking place in heaven at the end of time. Daniel 8:14 indicates that the judgment began in heaven in 1844 (see Lesson 22, "The 2,300-Day Prophecy").
   • cf. Revelation 11:18, 19. The judgment takes place while there are people living on the earth.
   • cf. Revelation 20:11, 12. We are judged by the deeds we have done as recorded in God's book of life.

5. **1 Peter 4:17.** The judgment begins with the investigation of the lives of God's people.

6. **Ecclesiastes 12:14.** Nothing will be missed or over-looked.
   - cf. Matthew 12:36, 37.
   - cf. 1 Corinthians 4:5.

7. **Exodus 32:31-33.** It is possible that some who have once accepted Jesus and whose names have been written in His book of life will have their names blotted out of His book because they have turned from Him to a life of sin.

8. **James 2:12.** God's law will be the standard of the judgment.
   - cf. Ecclesiastes 12:13.
   - cf. Revelation 22:14.

9. **Hebrews 7:25.** All of us are guilty of breaking God's law (cf. Romans 3:23; 6:23), so our only means of salvation in the judgment is to hide our lives in Christ, our Intercessor. His righteousness will cover us.
   - cf. 1 John 2:1.
   - cf. Colossians 3:3.
   - cf. Matthew 10:32.

10. **Revelation 3:5, 20.** Jesus appeals to us to invite Him into our hearts and let Him live out His life in us—before the verdict of the judgment is pronounced.

J-End.

# Baptism

*Marking Code: B*
*Marking Color: Blue*
*Key Text: Ephesians 4:3-5*

1. **Ephesians 4:3-5.** The Bible teaches one form of baptism. Baptism by immersion commemorates Jesus' death, burial, and resurrection. But Satan has a counterfeit for every truth of God—including a multiplicity of methods of baptism. Pouring, sprinkling, and other methods have been introduced into the church. But the important question is: What does the Bible say?

2. **Colossians 2:12.** Complete burial (immersion) under the water is the biblical method of baptism that accurately symbolizes our death and burial to sin. The Greek word *baptizo* means "to dip" or "to plunge under."
   - cf. John 3:23. John baptized where there was "much water" (so he could completely immerse those he baptized).
   - cf. Matthew 3:16. Jesus "came up immediately from the water" after His baptism.
   - Acts 8:38, 39. Philip baptized the Ethiopian by immersion.

3. **John 3:5.** Baptism is essential to salvation.
   - cf. Mark 16:16
   - cf. 1 Peter 3:21.

4. **Romans 6:3, 4.** Baptism symbolizes Jesus' death for

sin, burial, and resurrection. We die to sin, are buried beneath the waters of baptism, and are raised up out of the water to live a new life in Christ. Only baptism by immersion can truly symbolize the meaning of this ceremony.

5. **Matthew 28:19, 20.** Proper instruction and preparation of the heart need to take place before a person is baptized. The preparation includes understanding God's will for us, accepting Jesus as Savior, repentance for sin, a desire to be obedient to God's will, and a change in the life. For this reason, infant baptism is contrary to the Bible and the practice of the Early Church.
   • cf. Mark 16:16.
   • cf. Acts 8:35-37.

6. **Acts 2:38.** The Holy Spirit is evident in our lives when we are baptized and "put on" Christ.
   • cf. Galatians 3:26, 27.

7. **Acts 19:1-5.** When a person receives significant new light from God, re-baptism may be appropriate.

8. **Mark 1:9-11.** Jesus set the example for us by being baptized at the beginning of His ministry.
   • cf. 1 Peter 2:21.
   • cf.1 John 2:6.

9. **Acts 22:16.** A person should not delay when the proper time comes for baptism.

10. **1 Corinthians 12:12, 13.** We are invited to enter into the fellowship of one body in Christ through baptism.

   B-End.

# The Communion Service

*Marking Code: C*
*Marking Color: Black*
*Key Text: 1 Corinthians 11:23-30*

1. **1 Corinthians 11:23-30.** The bread and wine of the Communion service commemorate the great sacrifice of Jesus—His life of obedience and His death on the cross as an unblemished sacrifice for our sins. By celebrating the Lord's Supper we keep in mind His death and perfect atonement until He comes again.
   - cf. Matthew 26:26-30.
   - cf. Luke 22:14-20.

   **Note:** Paul makes several points regarding the Lord's Supper—or Communion. He says:
   - All who believe may eat the bread and drink the wine.
   - Spiritual preparation of the heart is necessary before taking part.
   - The Lord's Supper looks backward to Jesus' sacrifice and forward to the great marriage supper of the Lamb in heaven.
   - No set time is specified; some churches celebrate the Lord's Supper each quarter—four times per year.

2. **1 Corinthians 5:7, 8.** Leaven (yeast) and fermentation are symbols of sin and decay. Therefore, the bread used in the Communion service should be unleav-

ened bread, and the wine should not be fermented wine, but the pure juice of the grape. Only such symbols can accurately represent the perfect, unblemished sacrifice of Jesus.
- cf. 1 Peter 1:19; 2:22.

3. **Hebrews 10:10-14.** Christ died once as a complete, sufficient sacrifice. It isn't necessary to repeat His sacrifice over and over again as it is believed happens in the service of the mass. Communion is a symbolic remembrance of Jesus' sacrifice for us.

4. **John 13:1-17.** Jesus also instituted the service of foot washing as a preparation for the Lord's Supper.

   **Note:** The foot-washing service is important as a preparation for the Lord's Supper because of:
   - Christ's command—cf. John 13:14.
   - Christ's example—cf. John 13:15.
   - Christ's promised blessing—cf. John 13:17.

5. **Luke 22:16, 18.** The Communion service looks forward to the marriage supper of the Lamb which we will eat together with Jesus in heaven.
   - cf. Luke 12:37.

C-End.

# The Remnant Church

*Marking Code: R*
*Marking Color: Black*
*Key Text: Revelation 12:1*

1. **Revelation 12:1.** The history of the Christian church is outlined in the prophecy of Revelation 12. Symbolic prophecy is used, not to mystify, but to make plain. The Bible also provides a key to unlock the meaning of the symbols used. This helps to resolve many of the perplexities about the book of Revelation.

2. **Jeremiah 6:2.** God's people—the "daughter of Zion"—is compared to a lovely, delicate woman. The character of the woman indicates the character of the church being represented. A pure woman represents a church that is faithful to its Lord. An impure woman (cf. Revelation 17:3-5) represents a fallen church.
   • cf. 2 Corinthians 11:2

3. **Revelation 12:2-6, 13, 14.** Satan attempted to destroy the Christ child and the Early Church through Rome—in both its pagan and papal phases. Rome forced God's remnant church into exile.

4. **Revelation 12:15, 16.** Persecution during the Dark Ages (A.D. 538-1798) was accomplished by a flood of false doctrine that nearly obliterated God's true church. When the Reformation made clear many for-

gotten truths, Satan relaunched his attack on God's remnant church.

5. **Revelation 12:17.** The Bible gives two identifying characteristics of God's remnant church in the last days: it will keep God's commandments, and it will have the testimony of Jesus.

6. **Proverbs 4:18.** God wants us today to rediscover neglected truth that has been hidden so that our walk with Him will grow ever clearer and brighter as we follow His truth.

R-End.

# God's Gathering Call

*Marking Code: GC*
*Marking Color: Green*
*Key Text: Revelation 17:1-5*

1. **Revelation 17:1-5.** The impure woman of Revelation 17 is the opposite of the pure woman of Revelation 12. The pure woman represents God's faithful remnant church; the impure woman represents a false church. Satan's counterfeit of truth is Babylon—a fit name for the confusion of present-day worldly churches.
   • cf. Genesis 11:9. Babel (Babylon) originated in a confusion of languages.

2. **Revelation 17:6, 9, 15-18.** This chapter identifies a large, powerful, religious-political system of false worship ruling the world from Rome.

3. **Revelation 16:13, 19.** Babylon is made up of three parts—paganism, Romanism, and apostate Protestantism.
   • cf. Revelation 14:8.

4. **Revelation 18:1-4.** God invites the honest in heart to leave the fallen churches of the world and unite themselves with His faithful remnant people in keeping His commandments.
   • cf. Revelation 14:12.
   • cf. Revelation 12:17.

5. **John 10:27.** Christ's true sheep hear the call of the Good Shepherd. His obedient people will come out of Babylon—the fallen churches—into the faithful flock of the remnant who keep God's commandments.

6. **Matthew 12:30.** Just before the end of the world there will be no neutral ground. One must either stay in Babylon and be destroyed (cf. Revelation 18:8, 21) or be a part of God's remnant church and be saved for eternity (cf. Revelation 14:4, 5; 15:2, 3).

7. **Genesis 19:15-26.** It is as important for us to respond today and be obedient to God as it was for Lot to flee from ancient Sodom.

   GC-End.

# The Three Angels' Messages

## Lesson 28

*Marking Code: TA*
*Marking Color: Green*
*Key Text: Revelation 14:6-12*

1. **Revelation 14:6-12.** In every epoch of human history, God has given individuals the opportunity to accept the Savior, faithfully warning them of coming judgments and providing a way of escape. Before the end of time, God gives His last warning to earth's final generation. This warning is portrayed in Revelation 14 as messages from three angels flying in the sky.

2. **Revelation 14:6, 7.** The first angel proclaims:
   - the everlasting gospel. Since the Garden of Eden there has always been only one true gospel—salvation by grace. cf. Genesis 3:15; Mark 16:15; Acts 4:12.
   - the hour of God's judgment has come. cf. Daniel 8:14. This judgment began in 1844 at the close of the 2,300-day prophecy.
   - the need to worship God and give Him glory as the Creator. The seventh-day Sabbath points us to God as the Creator and re-Creator of our lives. cf. Exodus 20:8-11. We give Him glory by worshiping Him on the day He has set aside as His holy Sabbath day.

3. **Revelation 14:8.** The second angel proclaims:

- Babylon has fallen. Babylon represents spiritual apostasy and confusion. It is the opposite of God's faithful, last-day remnant church. cf. Revelation 18:1-4.

4. **Revelation 14:9-11.** The third angel proclaims:
   - that the "beast"—the power opposed to God in the last days—has a mark that denotes its authority. This mark involves a counterfeit day of worship in distinction to the Creator's seventh-day Sabbath. cf. Revelation 13:6, 16, 17; Daniel 7:25. Those who accept this mark give their allegiance to the beast.
   - a warning against receiving the mark of the beast, i.e., accepting any man-made system of false worship.
   - the strongest warning to be found anywhere in the Bible.

5. **Revelation 14:12.** The purpose of these three angels' messages is to warn us of error and identify truth. Those who accept this final warning from God constitute a worldwide movement of people from all religious faiths who follow God's Word.

6. **Revelation 22:14.** God's faithful people will give Him their loyalty and be obedient to His commandments.

TA-End.

# The Spirit of Prophecy

*Marking Code: SP*
*Marking Color: Green*
*Key Text: Amos 3:7*

1. **Amos 3:7.** God has promised to make known to us, through His prophets, anything that will significantly affect us and our relationship with Him. God's method of communication through His prophets is needed until the end of time in order to edify, strengthen, and build up His church.
   - cf. Ephesians 4:8-15. The gift of prophecy is to be in the church as long as we are growing into the fullness of Christ.
   - cf. Acts 2:17, 18.

2. **Revelation 12:17.** The "testimony of Jesus" is one of the identifying marks of God's faithful remnant church in the last days.

3. **Revelation 19:10.** The testimony of Jesus is the "spirit of prophecy."

4. **1 Thessalonians 5:20, 21.** We are not to despise prophecies, but we are to test them to determine if they truly come from God.
   - cf. 1 John 4:1-3.

5. **1 Corinthians 14:32.** No true prophet disagrees with previous prophecies of God.

- cf. 2 Peter 1:21.

**Note:** Spiritual tests of a true prophet include:
- cf. Isaiah 8:20. Their prophecies will be in harmony with the Bible.
- cf. Jeremiah 1:7; Deuteronomy 18:18-22. They will speak God's words—not their own opinions.
- cf. Jeremiah 28:9. Their predictions will be accurate and actually happen.
- cf. 1 John 4:2. They will exalt Christ in their messages.
- cf. Matthew 7:15-20. Their life and work will be exemplary and will rightly represent Christ.

**Note:** Physical tests of a prophet while in vision include:
- cf. Acts 10:10, 11. A trancelike state.
- cf. Numbers 24:2-4. The eyes remain open, but do not see the physical world around them.
- cf. Daniel 10:17. No breath while in vision.
- cf. Daniel 10:8. Natural strength departs.
- cf. Daniel 10:11, 18. Supernatural strength follows.

6. **Hosea 12:10, 13.** As ancient Israel was brought out of Egypt by a prophet, so God will again lead His people out of end-time Babylon by a prophet.

7. **2 Chronicles 20:20.** God promises spiritual prosperity if we believe His prophets.

**Note:** Seventh-day Adventists believe that the gift of prophecy is evidenced in the writings and work of Ellen G. White. Those who have carefully studied her writings can attest to their inspiration. She met every spiritual and physical test of a prophet.

Ellen G. White lived from 1827 until 1915. Although she had only three grades of formal education, she wrote some 100,000 manuscript pages on a wide variety of subjects. Her writings continue to withstand the test of time. Specialists in various fields who have examined what she wrote have testified that she was given knowledge far in advance of the times in which she lived.

Her work in the remnant church included more than the office of prophet. She championed reforms in health, temperance, medical, educational, and even orphanage work.

Her writings are designed to lead people back to the Bible, not to take the place of the Bible.

SP-End.

# The Seven Last Plagues

*Marking Code: P*
*Marking Color: Purple*
*Key Text: Revelation 15:5-8*

1. **Revelation 15:5-8.** John describes seven plagues that will fall on the earth just before Jesus returns. These plagues are the result of the widespread sin and disregard of God that will exist in the world at the end of time. They are God's wrath poured out against sin. When the divine decree goes forth that probation has ended for every person (cf. Revelation 22:14), God's strange act of destruction begins and punishment is poured out upon those who have defied God.

2. **Revelation 16:1, 2.** The first plague is a terrible sore that falls on those who receive the mark of the beast or worship his image.

3. **Revelation 16:3.** The second plague turns the seas of earth to blood.

4. **Revelation 16:4-7.** The third plague turns the rivers and springs of water to blood.

5. **Revelation 16:8, 9.** Under the fourth plague, the sun scorches human beings with extreme heat.

6. **Revelation 16:10, 11.** The fifth plague involves a heavy darkness—both spiritual and physical.

7. **Revelation 16:12-16.** The sixth plague initiates the battle of Armageddon. Under three camps, the entire rebellious world is gathered to receive God's judgment.

8. **Revelation 16:17-21.** The seventh plague marks the end of the great controversy between good and evil. Under this plague, Babylon falls and the earth is ravaged by hail and a great earthquake. These are the last convulsions of nature just before Jesus returns.

9. **Isaiah 33:14-16.** The seven last plagues fall on the wicked—those who have rejected God and His truth. During this time, God will protect and sustain His righteous people who trust Him.

10. **Psalm 91:1-16.** Every Christian can claim this song of assurance and deliverance.

    P-End.

# The Unpardonable Sin

## Lesson 31

*Marking Code: US*
*Marking Color: Black*
*Key Text: Matthew 12:31, 32*

1. **Matthew 12:31, 32.** Is there a sin that God cannot forgive? An unpardonable sin? The context of Matthew 12:31, 32 indicates that "blasphemy against the Spirit" means to speak hurtfully against the Holy Spirit. This sin is also called "the sin leading to death" (cf. 1 John 5:16, 17), and "presumptuous" sin or "great transgression" (cf. Psalm 19:13).

2. **1 Samuel 16:14.** As a result of this sin, we lose the Holy Spirit's presence and influence in our lives. Our conscience is anesthetized.
   - cf. 1 Timothy 4:2.

3. **1 John 1:7, 9.** There is no sin that God cannot forgive—provided we meet the conditions for forgiveness. Whatever sin we have committed, if we repent and confess it, God has promised to forgive us.
   - cf. Proverbs 28:13.

4. **John 16:8-11, 13.** The work of the Holy Spirit is to bring conviction of sin and lead us to confess and forsake our sins.
   - cf. John 14:16-18, 26.

5. **Ephesians 4:30.** We can grieve the Holy Spirit if we persistently harden our hearts to resist Him.
   - cf. Acts 7:51.
   - cf. Hebrews 3:7, 8.

6. **Hebrews 10:26, 29.** The unpardonable sin—the sin God cannot forgive—is the sin that we don't want pardoned! The only sin that cannot be forgiven is the sin for which we refuse to ask forgiveness. There is no sacrifice—forgiveness—for willful sin that we cherish and for which we refuse to confess and repent and ask forgiveness. God finally gives us up to our tragic choice.
   - cf. Proverbs 29:1.
   - cf. Romans 1:24.

7. **Hebrews 12:14-17.** It is possible to insist on choosing darkness to the point that eventually a person cannot repent—even if he wants to. The will has become set on sin.

8. **Psalm 51:11.** We need to pray daily for the gift of the Holy Spirit in our lives.
   - cf. Luke 11:13.

9. **2 Corinthians 6:2.** The time to respond to the leading of the Spirit is today—now!
   - cf. John 6:37.

US-End.